ONE BIRD FLYING

Monica Ditmas

Anima Poetry Press

First Published in 2016 by:

Anima Poetry Press
Cissbury
Ashfield Road
Midhurst
West Sussex
GU29 9JS

Cover image copyright © 2016 Lynne Ashcroft
Typset and Bound by Otter Bookbinding Ltd.

ISBN: 978-0-9935966-1-2

For Sheila and Hugh

Contents

Thoughts From the Village

Thoughts from Milkwood

Part 1

Thoughts From the Village

I retired to the beautiful village of Buriton after a busy career. This group of poems reflects my thoughts about how change affects us and considers physical and mental freedom.

LATE SNOW

Uninvited, a frozen cloud
settling upon a yellow drift
of daffodils, dares to re-arrange,
subtly, the April data.
We no longer know
where the roads are, but know
where the badger is, the wayfarer,
the escaped convict, the fox.
Spring water-colours give way
to sculpture. Noises are small
and precious, the lone blackbird
supplanting the lorry.
Hill farms are cut off
from the world by a white
desert, while lake shores
are joined by sudden bridges.
Human beings do not escape
the confusion, losing the certainties
of age. Children of four and forty
compete for toboggans,
while the aged, seven and seventy
whimper with cold, rubbing
their starved fingers, mourning
the loss of the green days.

Data Processing

Dawn. The day's computers
are switched on. Subconsciously
men sort and file their dreams
in deep lockers. Green plants
tune in to photo-system one,
harvesting the red light
of early morning. Busy screens
record the shock waves advancing
from suburbia, engulfing the city.

Within the brain the data
jostle painfully, overloading
the circuit. Fused minds
resort to the neutrality
of cigarettes, or coffee.
Among the survivors
some few courageously
confront the disorder
with a quiet analysis
they call prayer.

The Swimmer
For Michelle my Australian Grand-Daughter

Life goes on around me and I
swim. My passage through life
I can't control, but in the water
I make my own path with long, clean strokes.

The pool's green-blue mists part
and close behind me, accepting
my smooth limbs as I pass,
unsplashing, controlled, fish-finned with pleasure.

I know that the time must come
for darker waters, the cold salt waves,
the foam, the currents. Already
I see distanced the eddies where others

swim to survive. But I will put on
my life-jacket of memories, yes, will know
the tested strength, the serenity
learned in the green pools of my youth.

CANDLES

Candles.
Elongated lilies.
Or squat and red
cheekily burning.
I have filled the house
with their unreal
beautiful light.
And now I wish
there were power cuts always.
I wish
there were no strident days
following with loud laughter
and white unshadowed noons.

Now the invaded rooms
are a universe, filled
with separate wavering stars.
Chairs and tables assume
mysterious global outlines
of planets, orbital.
I think they are not
in their accustomed places,
while round them and above
our threaded memories move
filling with quiet delight
the inter-stellar spaces.

The Gallery

Looking back in old age at all the
loves and friendships of a long life.

Adding a friend
to a private collection
is at first simple,
the walls uncluttered.
The lay-out fluid, the fixings
haphazard. Some tacked up
unframed, for a few colourful weeks,
others driven in recklessly
with six-inch nails, their removal
leaving a mark for life.

Later the portraits
winnowed and sifted, acquire
their permanent settings, each
adjusted to its neighbours,
listed and catalogued,
though a few always
persist aggressively in the wrong room,
oil with water-colour,
gouache with pencil,
the symmetry of the whole
just less than perfect.

At this late stage
adding to the collection
becomes a rare, expensive
exercise in love,

not likely to occur
unless compulsively, the interest
of the subject *per se*,
and its treatment, leaving no valid
alternative choice.

When all is done,
the carpenters dismissed,
the ledges dusted,
the connoisseur will walk
through the rooms daily,
regarding his life's treasures
with veneration and love.

Pausing before his early
acquisitions with amused
tranquil affection,
accepting with a wry smile
those he has never really been
sure of, the misfits,
the aberrations, those not normally
his kind of art.

But before this, his greatest,
most costly purchase,
he will stand still, the breath
coming slowly, the mind
emptied of comment, a slow tide
of awe engulfing the heart.

RYLAND ROAD

This poem is a tribute to my son Hugh, who at the time was living in what had once been a fairly prosperous district of Birmingham, but is now a very deprived area, just north of Spaghetti Junction, with continuous traffic noise day and night.

He sits on your front doorstep
blocking your way, as if it were
his house. He is old.
The black lustre drained from his skin
years ago, leaving him
with a grey mask the city
has fastened on him.

He sits as of right.
There is nowhere else to sit
in this long street
of railed-off houses.
It is only
because your fence is smashed
that he can sit here,
transforming the harsh welcome
you got when you moved in
from scar to sanctuary.

An elusive gleam of sun
catches him between roof-tops,
warm and good, well sun is sun
anywhere. He opens his hands.

I wait for your righteous indignation
as you finger a useless key.
But it seems that for you
there is no dilemma. It is simply
how life is arranged.
You say 'nice bit of sun'
and turn off down a side alley
to get home a back way,
climbing over a wall.

Whilst I, humbled, walk on
along the squalid pavement
of Ryland Road, feeling it
somehow redeemed,
the complexities of its suffering
simplified, your gentle acceptance
softening the hard stones.

My Garden

For Sheila

My garden. Mine, of course,
created to my design
from patches of rough grass
and rampant weeds, and paths
of linear ugliness, but now
smoothed into gentle curves,
with plants acquired from Kew
or Wisley, to flower in season
in continuous ordered beauty.

Yes, this garden was mine.
I never questioned my right
to keep this child always
under my strict control.
No teenage years permitted,
anything it did on its own
monitored, and if need be
erased, banished, denied.
Intruding friends not welcomed.
My vision had to be whole.

But now, in age, it seems
I've been obliged to concede
my garden's freedom to choose
its own unique display.
So now self-seeds prevail,
aquilegias smothering roses,
a single tall foxglove

erupting among the cornflowers,
bindweed, laughing and jeering,
entwining itself at will,
and lady's mantle attempting
to clothe the entire garden
with its delicate green-gold cape.

Now too the unplanned seasons
are sometimes a blaze of glory,
at other times a scene
of played-out drab exhaustion.
A bit like life really.
And a bit like me, so perhaps
truly appropriate, sharing
the random mix and muddle
of joy and deprivation
that constitutes old age.

Walking For Health

This poem was written on a day when I had coffee in the local Pop-In Centre, Winton House, and found it full of residents from a local residential home, taken out for a morning treat, most of them very elderly and infirm.

'Walking For Health' the latest poster says.
Grey heads are lifted, giving it brief scan,
then back to focus on the chequered cloth,
the buttered buns and fairy cakes and jam.
Redemption's more immediate and sure
when offered in such safe, familiar ways.

Photos of white-haired walkers fill the screen.
'This Might Be You' But no, they are not us.
Yes, they have sticks, but move with sprightly step
even on stony paths. We go by bus.
Or even ambulance. A waste of time
to fret for something that might once have been.

Yet, in her wheelchair, there is one, just one,
who keeps on gazing, silent, mesmerised
by memories of green hills, wild moors, white sands,
walking with Ben, on countless routes devised
to honour mountain peaks that bear his name –
Ben Eighe, Ben Lawes, Ben Nevis. Winter sun

melting the snow slopes. Sudden driving rain
deluging Gable's crags. A rolling mist
enveloping Cat Bells at early dawn.
And sun on Scafell Pike, where first they kissed,

and kissed again while making the descent,
and, after, celebrated with champagne.

Soon aching limbs return her to the room.
Bright yellow walls replace the arching sky,
gossip the whispering wind. Yet, hazy now,
with hectoring print the poster looms above.
Walking for health? How very strange that seems,
how pitiable, to one who walked for love.

THE TELESCOPE

FOR DAVID BEE

*This poem was written on Easter Day and simply
gives the Easter message – all is well.*

In grey dawns, I hold it.
In grey noontides, again
I take this undesired,
persistent telescope
to scan the deep horizons
of my own being. Where
are the stars, or maybe,
just maybe, even suns.

But dark, shrouding clouds
close down on meaner images,
drab moorlands, muddied fields,
confused contours, or at best,
an ordinariness of landscape,
unilluminated, altogether
an apology for mis-spent life.

But suddenly, gently, quietly,
the telescope is removed
from my faltering hands.
Someone has taken it from me,
turned it, turned it around.
Now from some unknown source
like sunrise from the east
a slanting light appears,
dimly at first, a copper glow,

then stronger, richer, warmer,
spreading like peaceful fire,
a golden alchemy
that turns the mud to star dust.

None of this is my doing.
So whose hands hold it now,
this upturned telescope?

I do not know, yet know.
I also know that I
can lie down safely now,
and sleep in joy and peace.

'THEY MIGHT COME IN'

IN MEMORY OF MY MOTHER

The hoard is growing. Endless cardboard boxes,
all shapes and sizes, with a knitted scarf
unused in years, plus battered picture frames,
some still containing sepia photos
of long-dead friends who used to make her laugh.

Her cupboards ache and groan. The bulging loft
is spared renewed invasion, since she can
no longer climb to it. It's now the floor
that bears the brunt, hosting a growing pile
of newspapers, worn slippers, cotton rags.
'They might come in, you never know, dear, do you?'
deflecting censure with a gentle smile.

I miss her as I go to throw away
useless possessions, her remembered voice
still playing in my head. At the same time
I know that I congratulate myself
on having settled for the better choice.

And yet I also have a precious hoard,
the words of poets, prophets. Some will say
they are outmoded, useless, that I am
sadly deluded in my estimate,
it's proven facts, not words, we need today.

Would it be sensible to disavow
the value of these sayings? 'When I tread
the valley of death's shadow, I will have
no fear, for you are with me.' Should I now
consign this, useless, to my memory's bin?
Again I hear that voice from long ago,
and speaking now with certainty, not hope.
'No, hold it fast! You'll find it will come in.'

Awakening

It's part of growing old, I guess,
that I'm awake by half-past five
and do not feel the former joy
of being vibrantly alive.

And yet I know that if I slept
I'd miss this miracle of sound,
this liquid song that's pouring out
from quivering bird-throats all around.

Why do they sing? They do not know.
They have no need to justify,
or find some cause for what they do.
Their lives are open to the sky.

Having no memory of pain
nor fear of what the day may bring,
seeing their world as born again,
what should they ever do but sing?

The Search

My father died when I was thirteen, leaving me
with an inadequate childish picture of him, rather
than a deep knowledge and understanding. Later
on in life I felt this as a sad lack.

Greedily sifting diaries
and bundled letters, I seek
the man with whom I share
genes but not memories.
Childhood cheated by death.

But facts disappoint, speaking
less surely than my own
implanted hungers; the need
for quietness, green spaces,
a craving for a few,
a precious few, loved faces.

It may be that you do
picture me still, an image taken
direct from life.
What is it that you see?
An eager, thin child's face,
with anxious eyes,
fearful of disapproval, yet aware
of inner certainties of joy?
Or she I have become, white-haired,
marked by my four-score years?

I hold your sepia photo, faded now.
Little enough to know you by – high forehead
and full mouth shyly set
emptied of speech. And yet your eyes
follow me as I move, with serious greeting,
steady and grave. Often indeed they seem
gently to smile, as if they knew the day
surely not far off now, of our next meeting.

The Sieve

This poem was written on Ash Wednesday, the first day of Lent.

I am old. I need to press
raspberries through a sieve
to eliminate hard pips
that spoil their eloquence,
leaving only scarlet goodness.

I do this also
for coarser things,
the rough skins of beans,
the fibres of celery.
What's left is simply
essence of usefulness.

I need also to sift
the contents of my mind.
but where is the filter,
the fine discerning mesh
to remove all ugliness,
all petty self-deceits,
all unforgiving judgments,
all ego-serving pride?
And would there then remain
the self that God created?

Where is this filter?
It is, alas, not thought.
Thinking cannot do it.
It just highlights the flaws.

God, I beseech you,
lean down from heaven
and pass your sieve to me.

Birthday Present

This poem commemorates my sister Dorothy
who lived in Buriton for many years.

They have dressed you in red
today, someone remembering
it was always your favourite colour
in those days (we have photos still)
when you took on the world.
That dress, on leave from the Wrens.
The outrageous hats that gave
the gossip columns their fill.

But now the flamboyance seems
an affront to your drooping head.
And the sleek red blouse at odds
with grey skin and straggly hair.
Your thin shoulders cry out
for a warm blanket instead.

We group ourselves round your chair,
vaguely aware that we're losing
all sense of why we are here.
Our cheerful attempts at greeting
founder on silence. The gifts
we took such trouble in choosing
evoke no response, not even
the child's book, big and bold,
which we thought might be just your line.
Rabbits, puppies and cats.
You remember your pets?

You loved them, didn't you?
But there's no answering sign.

Then suddenly you lean
slightly forward, your gaze
fixed on the paper wrapping
discarded upon the floor.
You stretch out a tentative hand
your eyes seeming to plead
I want it. Someone bends down
responding to this strange need.

You take it, regard it solemnly,
turn it over, drop it, and then
motion you want it back.
We watch with awe and surprise
as a gleam of understanding
dawns in your vacant eyes.

What is it you feel? The remembered
ecstasy of a three-year-old
shuffling through crumpled colours
on a bygone Christmas Day?
But no, it is more than this.
Somehow, it seems, you've been given
a miraculous birthday present,
a brief moment of bliss,

a moment, almost, of peace.
It's as if you suddenly knew
that what is left of you here

is just wrapping, paper thin,
whose usefulness soon will cease.
And in that merciful moment
you've also been made aware
that the gift that was once within
is not damaged or lost, but awaits you,
eternally safe, elsewhere.

Traffic Jam

The cortege winds ahead. Reluctant
mourners follow, not knowing
whose funeral it is, or whether
it is merely time being buried
in the wasted fumes and fret
of a savage summer.

Leaning out, I would pick
a wreath if I could. The verges
offer white dead-nettle, buttercup
and delicate spikes of sweet
vernal grass, fitting tribute
to hallow a coffin.

But each time that I almost touch
I am snatched away. Above us,
at a great height, a buzzard hovers,
mocking our impotence,
then flies off, his wings
drumming an elegy. The dead hours
must pass, otherwise, unlamented.

THE PARADOX

This poem started life in my head a year ago,
while I was still in my own home, but is
equally relevant in my thoughts today.

At aphelion, earth
yearns for the depth of space,
cursing the giant star
that keeps it in its place.

In rebellion, man
though at the last remove,
by gravitational plan
cannot escape God's love.

But here's the paradox
which faith and science, both
in their respective disciplines,
confirm to be the truth

that without these restrictions
all life would cease to be.
In fact we owe our freedom
to blessed captivity.

Part 2

THOUGHTS FROM MILKWOOD

*At the age of 92, failing health meant that I
had to leave my independent life and become a
resident of a care home called Milkwood. I had,
of course, brought my physical problems with
me and had lost much freedom but, at the same
time, had quickly realised how fortunate I was
to have found such a kind and loving new
home, where I would be safe and cared for.
Again I have recorded my thoughts
and emotions in poetry.*

The Inseparables

This poem was written about a week after I arrived at Milkwood House on January 27th 2016 and was coming to terms with the huge change of leaving my home. The inner tensions I describe apply at every stage of life, they were simply now heightened for a while, and I knew my destiny was in God's hands.

Everything intensified now,
the dark darker,
the light brighter.
More darkness, pain, confusion,
but light more glorious than ever;
beautiful beyond description.

My soul flits to and fro
between these two poles,
which ultimately are just one.
If I missed either experience
life would be incomplete.

If no darkness, I would not be able
to comprehend the full glory of light.
It would be nothing extraordinary.
Just taken for granted,
with me a mechanical puppet.

From creation onwards
both day and night,
blue skies and shadows.

No heaven without hell.
No resurrection without a cross.

I give thanks
that now, in this last phase
of my human existence,
I'm allowed to be aware
of this perfect one-ness of life.

Sleep

This was written ten days later and, of course, reflects the same tensions.

'Sleep' has gone to sleep tonight.
I can't wake him to help me.
'Can't sleep' has turned up instead,
unrepentant in his malignant activity.
However a third person,
a more beautiful bed-fellow,
whose name I don't know,
has also turned up, and has given me
a strategy to defeat him,
presenting me with a book
bound in gold
from the kingdom of memory.
And I may take it
and pick at random, replacing
worry with wonder.

So I recall
holding my children in my arms
a few minutes after their birth;
flying over Cairo
in an open cockpit Tiger Moth;
gazing in awe at the Southern Cross
gleaming brilliantly in a dark sky
halfway between Ayers Rock
and Alice Springs.

And beauty in words.
'Everyone suddenly burst out singing,
And I was filled with such delight
As prisoned birds must find in freedom
Winging wildly across the white
Orchards and dark green field;
On-on-and out of sight.'
Such memories as these
have power to heal the darkest
and longest hours of night.

Transit Camp

Written on a day when I was
very aware of human fragility.

I know I'm in a transit camp,
but not a refugee.
I do not flee my past.
It had its griefs and failures
but much was good for me.
I part with it serenely,
knowing it could not last.

And in this transit camp
I do not have to live
trapped in a tented city,
with meagre food to eat,
and not enough clean water,
perhaps compelled to witness
the suffering of a child,
someone's lost son or daughter.

Yet I am on the move
but not to a location
mapped on planet earth.
Not London town to Birmingham,
or Buriton to Liss.
This journey is quite different,
and cannot be recorded
in any travel journal.
It leads from what is temporal
to what will be eternal.

Today we have changing of towels

*The format of this poem is derived from one written by
Henry Reed concerning his experiences as a conscript in
World War 2, when being taught how to fire a rifle. It
was headed 'Today we have naming of parts'.*

Today we have changing of towels. Yesterday
we had checking of fire alarms. And tomorrow
it will be checking of weight, and this
done incomprehensibly, in kilos,
not in good old stones and pounds. But today
we have changing of towels. Daffodils
are tossing their golden heads in the garden,
dancing in a capricious lively wind.
And today we have changing of towels.

Soon we will have washing of feet. This
is quite possible for us to do
if we have enough strength
in our backs to lift them up higher
or bend down to reach them. In the garden
a pair of magpies are in flight, with flashes
of black and white brilliance, free
as birds you might say.
And today we have changing of towels.

RELOCATION

This poem was prompted by a notice on the staff room door: 'Please keep this door shut, as there are staff valuables/medication which could be relocated!'

As a child, I used, whenever
a chance arose, to relocate
some scrummy biscuits
from their official home
in a large tin downstairs
into a secret niche
contrived within my room,
which I hoped might be safe
from prying eyes and broom.
But if this was discovered
the punishment was only
a scolding, or at worst
a smack. So on the whole
I felt it was worth it.

As I grew older, of course,
I learned such relocation
to be a crime, often deserving
a prison sentence, the length
depending on the value
of the objects relocated
or the frequency of offence.
My earlier attitudes
had now to be revised.

This new moral teaching
made perfect legal sense.

But here at Milkwood, oddly,
normal allocations of guilt
appear to be reversed.
The blame of relocation
unfairly seems to fall
not on the offenders
but on the victims. They
will be the ones accursed
and find themselves in court
if the health of relocators
has been at any time
endangered by ingesting
the proceeds of their crime!

Temptation

*I don't think this is an unusual reaction. I once
had a pupil who had been stone deaf and when
finally this was cured by surgery burst into my
study weeping with horror and dismay.*

'He made the deaf to hear'
and they went away rejoicing
experiencing delight.
Life totally transformed,
a hundred new sensations
filling each eager head,
the sound of human voices,
trumpets, drums and birdsong
soft whispers of the wind.
For months I had been deaf,
so naturally I found
I'm longing for my date
with clever audiologists
swiftly to come around.

It does, and I return
with brand new hearing aids
more powerful than before.
I note the traffic round us
now does not glide by silently
but with a deafening roar.
And on my arrival
the voices all around

are not mouths moving gently
but deep confusing sound.

Back in my room the same.
The corridor outside
no longer flows silently
but also now provides
loud banging doors and chatter
and trolleys swishing by.
And voices on the telly
I hear them, yes, at last,
but still can't understand them
because they speak too fast.

And so I find myself
not delighted, but in pain,
and longing to be back
in blissful peace again,
spared all of this commotion.
And so there comes to me
a rather wicked notion.
Instead of being bothered
when people seem to shout,
I'll part with my new hearing aids
and take the wretches out!

Palm Sunday

*I gradually began to get over the shock of my
new situation and to observe my surroundings,
fellow residents and staff.*

Today for the first time
I ventured in my wheelchair
up to the floor above
to have my midday meal
with others, not alone.
It was a revelation
with dark blue linen napkins
and flowers on every table,
a dining room deserving
instant appreciation.

Yet it was deeply filled
with hush, a special sound,
not silence, but an ethos
heavy with thoughts unspoken
and the buried thoughts of many
for whom words are no longer
entirely useful: a hush
both moving and profound.

Today it is Palm Sunday,
and in this hush my thoughts
turn to a city elsewhere,
providing such contrast,
noisy with crowds applauding,
but with one silent figure

facing great suffering, removed
from all this briefly given
and spurious adulation,
just riding past.

I think he'd feel at home here,
him of no fixed abode,
and yes, the more I listen
to this hush, the more I sense
the presence of a donkey,
gentle, riding among us,
bearing his precious load.

THE LAST SUPPER

To-night is known as the night
of the Last Supper. But I note
the trays are coming round
as usual, with their varying loads
according to personal taste.
I detect no signs of anxiety,
foreboding or undue haste.

We know there'll be supper again
for all of us tomorrow.
If carers are anxious
they certainly do not show it.
Yet even here there may be
one person for whom this
is truth, as it was for one man
hundreds of years ago,
although, quite unlike him,
they may as yet not know it.

On this night by tradition
there is also washing of feet.
But such a symbolic gesture
cannot be needed here.
Carers wash feet every day,
faithful to their vocation.
They have no need to prove
that they are called to serve
by special demonstration.

Everything seems as usual.
Yet given all this, I sense
somehow a special quality
in the air tonight, a strange
infiltration of memories
in the quiet spaces above,
memories of an upper room
and that one man facing death
making a humble gesture
given on his knees,
to demonstrate infinite love.

DRESS REHEARSAL

All our staff were summoned on June 15th
at 7.00 pm for a special training exercise
supervised by a member of our local
Fire Brigade.

'All the world's a stage.'
Of course with the great bard
I cannot disagree.
But I have just been given
a stage that was unique,
provided just for me.
Here in my own large room
I've been allowed to view
the crucial Dress Rehearsal
of that great play 'Rescue',
with Milkwood House on fire
and all our spendid staff
seen at their very best,
fighting to bring to safety
each vulnerable guest.

In the first Act the focus
was clearly on a fragile
and nervous individual
who would quite meekly follow
any instructions given.
The actor who was chosen
to play this gentle part
came in to sit with me,

closing the door behind him.
We chatted as we waited
for the great play to start.

I must admit I think
they got the casting wrong!
He's a delightful person,
but very tall and strong,
able to cope with anything,
so when the rescuer came
it made her laugh to see
this person sitting there,
and consequently she
departed from her script,
and did not say the needed
calm words of reassurance
he was supposed to hear.

But Act 2 was quite brilliant!
The carer who came in
to wait for rescue here
behaved from her first entrance
in the aggressive manner
her script of course prescribed.
She did not speak to me,
removed her heavy boots
and flung them on the floor,
then without my permission
curled up upon my bed.

I recognised at once
a different challenge here!

And as might be expected
quite suddenly four carers
burst in, and went to lift her
to carry her away.
She put up a great fight,
struggling and kicking strongly,
before they got their way.
It made me laugh and laugh.
So now what can I say?
In the end I'm sure it's clear
the verdict has to be
the Rehearsal was successful –
And a great treat for me!

A Fellow Guest

In care homes many residents suffer from
dementia. Bedroom doors are not locked.

I have a new found friend
just along the corridor,
who wanders in to see me
many times each day
and often too at night.
Her gentle face retains
traces of former beauty
and her designer clothes
suggest an affluent past.
But now she's always haunted
by an enduring sense
of being trapped, imprisoned.
Her whole being speaks
of fear and of frustration.
Against these present sufferings
her past, however fortunate,
can offer no defence.

She's desperate to get out,
perhaps to shop at Tesco's
or visit her dear mother
who is now, or so she thinks,
aged about eighty-seven.
I tell her that probably
she has no need to worry,

her mother is well and happy
and safely held in heaven.

'Heaven' is a word
she at once understands.
She tells me of her grandfather
who was a well-known preacher.
Then suddenly a smile!
She remembers her small grandson
hiding in a church
behind the altar cloth.
Everyone looks for him
and suddenly he jumps out
and shouts triumphantly
'Here I am! I'm here!'
But, alas, the smile soon fades
and joy again gives way
to a permanence of fear.

CONVERSATION

This piece of nonsense cannot be called a poem and
has no respect for punctuation as this would not
bother an ant would it

A little black creature
suddenly appeared from nowhere
running along the rim
of my supper tray

I said to him
are you a flea
he said no I'm an ant
I said to him I'm sorry
I think I must kill you
he said come on
aren't you british
where is the fair play
I'm much smaller than you are

I said well but look
at the difference in numbers
I bet you are not
the only one of your species
here living with us
there are probably hundreds
I am greatly outnumbered
I think I must kill you

by this time he was
about to run off my tray

so I could not give him
a chance to reply
I went with all speed
to use a handy thumb
to do this dire deed
I feel that this action
was not really bad
and yet all the same
poor little creature
I feel a bit sad

FULL CIRCLE

FOR LIANNE

'In my beginning is my end.
In my end is my beginning.'
T.S.ELIOT

I'm a child, I live
in a world full of wonder.
Those bright twinkling stars
hanging up there.
What holds them up?
I have no idea.
In the garden I have
my own secret pathway,
weaving darkly
between the tall shrubs.
I can crawl through
where no one can see.
This path is known only
to the cat and to me.

Behind the gooseberry bushes
fairies are dancing
hand in hand with each other.
Unwisely, I mention this
to my strict grandmother.
She doesn't quite say so
but she thinks I tell lies.
Grown-ups can't see them,

and they can't see angels.
I have different eyes.

As I grow older
slowly but surely
reason takes over.
There's no longer a heaven
above the blue sky.
Science, technology
hold the world's future.
In fact, given time
our minds are so clever
we may be on course
to explain the whole universe
and mystery will vanish
for ever and ever.

But at age of ninety-two
childhood starts to return.
Reason, intellect, logic –
it's their turn to fade.
I slowly recover
that previous dimension
of marvel and mystery
so long overlaid.

WHICH?

I am in the ring of life,
but laid back, not fighting,
out for the count.

How many counts are left?
And who is counting?
Will the verdict be
you should summon up all your strength,
get up and go on?

Or, it is fine, you may
lie there, not observing
any observers, lie there
in blissful peace?

LEAF FALL

October 2016: Nature at its most perfect?

Autumn. The trees prepare
to discard their green leaf offspring
who have now served their purpose,
though only eight months old.
They do it with panache,
robing them in glory
with scarlet and with gold.

And when the leaves are gone
the trees reveal their skeletons
to be also things of beauty,
with curving arms outstretched
and delicate hands and fingers,
each with its own design,
a gallery of etchings
pencilled upon the sky.

Gifts

When politicians admit to changing their minds
they are howled down with cries that they should
resign. But surely it is important not to get closed
minds in life, and for me that includes all aspects
including faith. I think it is essential for all growth
and a big change like moving here from home is
bound to stimulate the process. Hence
this poem.

God hands out his pearls
of insight in sequence,
but of each he may say
'Give it back'
before he will deliver the next.
So sometimes there is
a gap between gifts,
and the jewels
are hard to part with,
for each time I believe
I have the full truth
that will last for ever.

But faith, it seems,
has no resting places.
There is always space ahead.
And so there are times
when I have only
a space on my finger,
a stoneless ring,

to remind me of Him.
I have to trust
that when pain comes, or death,
whether I have or have not
at that moment, the pearl
and its absence count equally
as tokens of love.

Time

November 2016

In my old age I discover
I have a remarkable choice.
I can live life as normal
with its expected framework
of past, present, future,
or switch to a different mode
where life has just one voice.

Then it's as if I'm sitting
at the keyboard of a piano,
childish trebles at one end,
deeper notes at the other,
and can press any key at will
since I am in control.
Events are no longer tied
to fixed dates in the calendar,
and life becomes not a sequence
but just a single whole.

In the first mode I treasure
my photos of my mother.
In the second I don't need them
seeing her actual face,
and when I press the keys
the sounds that can be heard
are not merely recordings
but are as fresh and clear
as the live song of a bird.

It seems that Thomas Hardy
also experienced this,
writing that 'time shakes
this fragile frame at eve
with throbbings of noontide'.
But then he would switch back
into conventional thinking,
of past, present and future,
and sometimes give us verses
which break our hearts to read.
'Death will not appal
one who, past doubtings all,
waits in unhope'.
To wait without hope must be
a tragedy indeed.

But there's another poet
for whom a major theme,
often in verse sublime,
runs throughout all his work —
the timelessness of time.
'The moment of the rose
and the moment of the yew tree
are of the same duration.'
But unlike his fellow poet,
T S Eliot looks ahead
not with despair or doubt
but with fervent expectation.

My verdict goes with him,
to look ahead with hope.
It seems that humans can
in their last years on earth
receive a special blessing,
this second mode of viewing,
a sort of partial preview
of what it will be like
to move from what is temporal,
when the right time has come,
to what will be eternal.

ONE BIRD FLYING

*I managed to be taken in my wheel chair to the
memorial service for my dearest lifelong friend Leslie
in the village where we both used to live and before
she died she had asked that this poem of mine should
be read. I have never had any idea where the last
three lines of this poem emerged from and have not
known what they meant. A friend read it for me and
suddenly in this setting the meaning became clear, not
only for me but for all present. It describes the flight of
the soul as it leaves this world for the next, a journey
we all have to take alone.*

Slowly, distantly, the trees
waken to April sun.
Above them, drifting clouds
dispense alternate streams
of light and shadow,
flowing across the green
of spring foliage, gilding
and darkening, gilding
with gold-leaf, darkening
with green-black caverns.

Silently, the clouds
traverse the endless sky
in shifting patterns.
No other movement is there
until, slowly,
across the vast spaces

one tiny shape moves, silhouetted,
alone in the universe.

One bird flying.
O my soul!
One small bird flying.